Make Money The New Fashion Way 2.0

Make Money The New Fashion Way 2.0

This Revolution Will Not Be Televised

Ruben Cobos

© 2016 Rapacious Dimenphetic Inc.
All rights reserved.
Cover design by Bruce Muniz of Bamboo Graphics
Light bulb and gears image created by Maksym Yemelyanov

ISBN-13: 9780997344516
ISBN-10: 0997344512
Library of Congress Control Number: 2016945079
Rapacious Dimenphetic Inc, Staten Island, NY

Special thanks to Antonia Tamburello and Bruce Muniz for always believing in me and all of my projects. You are amazing, and I really appreciate you!

Message to Readers

This is not a coincidence or an accident that you are reading this. This is the law of attraction working its magic. Somehow, someway, we both manifested this day. You are never alone.

Ruben Cobos

Table of Contents

Message to Readers · · · · · · · · · · · · · · · · · · vii

Chapter 1   The Epiphany · 1

Chapter 2   State of Emergency · · · · · · · · · · · · · · · · · · 8

Chapter 3   Entrepreneurship · · · · · · · · · · · · · · · · · · · 16

Chapter 4   Network Marketing · · · · · · · · · · · · · · · · · 23

Chapter 5   Prospecting · 32

Chapter 6   Present the Opportunity · · · · · · · · · · · · · · 40

Chapter 7   Fortune Is in the Follow-Up · · · · · · · · · · · · 47

Chapter 8	The Decision	58
Chapter 9	Mentoring	64
Chapter 10	The Journey	72
Affirmation Bonus Chapter I Am the Force		79

Notes	109
About the Author	113

1

THE EPIPHANY

A Need

A FEW YEARS AGO, I felt as if somehow I was running out of time—as if time was just speeding by, and I was getting older and couldn't do anything about it. My life seemed to be nothing but work. I was working in sales, management, and consulting, and I was working multiple jobs. What I needed, very badly, was more time back in my life without sacrificing my positive cash flow. I felt that with more spare time and more control over my life, I would be happier and more fulfilled. I was working around the clock and had very little social life. I wanted a wife and a family. Also, I wanted to spend more time with my family, including my grandmother, who was getting older. My concerns included my physical, mental, spiritual, emotional, and social well-being. After realizing that I had several needs that were not being fulfilled and that my life was passing me by, I began meditating and praying. My prayers and meditations became a focal point in my life; I hoped that with enough prayer, deep thought, contemplation, and meditation, I could figure something out. Trust me when I say that this was not an easy process. Some nights, I would literally toss and turn, trying to go to sleep but unable to, desperately hoping that I could gain more control over my life and my time and that I could gain more fulfillment as well. I went from having a vague sense of unease with my life situation to finally realizing exactly what my problems were to then feeling very strongly that I had no choice but to get control of my life.

Epiphany

One Saturday morning, after months of trying to figure things out, I woke up at 5:30 a.m. with an epiphany; the solution that I needed had been right under my nose for several years. I just had to make the connection. I went to my laptop and typed in the name of a company from which I had been buying products for several years. I understood their product and how well it worked, but after watching several YouTube videos, I also began to understand how their business model worked and that it could work to solve my problems. This company used a business model called network marketing, which I will explain in much more detail shortly. After realizing that I wanted to get involved, I signed up under a distributor of this product online. By this time it was still only 6:00

a.m., so it was too early to call anyone. I was charged up. I called a couple of my best friends when the time was reasonable. I explained what I had discovered. My friends agreed to sign up as distributors of this product under me and did the same with their friends, so we made progress together.

In the weeks that followed, I began selling this product to many people, including many of the contacts I had built up. My friends did the same, and I was making progress. Not long after that, an executive from this company called me because she could tell how strong my sales were online, and she wanted to know what I was doing. She put me on a three-way call with an even higher-level executive, an "upline," who explained that over seven years, he had cleared $1 million by signing up more and more people under him to distribute this company's product. He had signed up 323 people to his independent-distributor website, and then they signed up people under him, so he served as an upline to more than seventeen thousand people. Basically, he had signed up four people a month for seven years as distributors under him, netting $1 million. I asked some questions, he gave me a list of things to do, and I got started. After hearing how I could achieve financial and time freedom, I decided I was in. This was exactly what I needed!

Taking Action

After deciding I was fully in, I worked really hard at learning all of the intricacies of network marketing, which is really an exciting method of earning money. I read and studied books and other materials, attended events, and participated in calls with prospects and with experts. In addition, I made a comprehensive list of all of my contacts, including their e-mail addresses and phone numbers, to develop my prospect list. During this time, I also attended events at which successful people went onstage to explain how they had effectively gained control over their lives and financial freedom with network marketing. Through network marketing, in which I am very involved, I have found a better way to make a living, and I have not looked back!

2

STATE OF EMERGENCY

The Economy

Before we get into some of the problems with the economy, jobs, and debt, let us consider one interesting statistic. The movie industry, the music industry, and the NFL are huge moneymakers, with the movie industry bringing in around $80 billion a year, the music industry bringing in approximately $16 billion a year, and the NFL earning approximately $9 billion per year. On the other hand, consider that network marketing, brings in the almost unthinkable amount of around $178 billion a year globally. This means that there are positives in the economy and endless possibilities with network marketing, which we will explore in much more detail.

In the United States today, however, there are real problems that cause concern and that indicate we are in a state of emergency. Big businesses across the country have outsourced jobs to other countries in the past few decades, which leaves fewer jobs available. In addition, companies routinely lay off employees as they face decreasing profits or when they simply want to increase their profits as much as possible. One indication that the economy is in bad shape is that the number of people on food stamps and other types of government assistance has been steadily increasing over the past few years. Some people who are employed on a part-time or even a full-time basis do not make enough money to pay their bills, so they must rely on food stamps and other types of government assistance, which relates to the poor shape of the American economy and the real unemployment rate. Also, the average salaries of workers in the United States, including those with college degrees, are, generally speaking, either declining or, at best, not keeping up with the rising cost of living.

The Real Unemployment Rate

According to the federal government's Bureau of Labor Statistics, the country's unemployment rate had declined to a mere 5.3 percent as of June 2015. This is not, however, the real unemployment rate, due to several factors. First, this does not include people who work on a part-time basis or who pick up an occasional work assignment here and there. In other words, people who are underemployed, even so much so that they are essentially unemployed, are not counted as unemployed people. Second, many unemployed people are able to receive unemployment benefits for a few months. While the actual number of months they are eligible to receive unemployment varies from state to state, the fact is that once a person's unemployment benefits run out, that person is no longer counted as being unemployed, even if he or she has not yet found a job. Third, people who are discouraged by their lack of prospects and have stopped trying to find work are also not counted by the Department of Labor in unemployment statistics.

Because of these facts, it is estimated that around thirty million Americans who should be able to be working (not including those who are too young to work, disabled, or past retirement age) are underemployed or out of work altogether. In June of 2015, the rate of labor force participation was

62.6 percent, which meant that 37.4 percent of the people in America who could and should be employed were not working or actively seeking employment. All of this goes to show that the actual rate of unemployment in America is much higher than the federal government claims it is.

Debt in America

There is a good reason that so many people talk and complain about the level of debt in America. It is unprecedented and rising steadily. The national debt is currently more than $18 trillion! The amount of money that people owe for student loans taken out to attend college is more than $1 trillion. (Keep in mind that most student loan debt, under current laws, cannot be discharged in bankruptcy, unlike other types of unsecured debt.) Private debt, the cumulative debt that all Americans have together, is more than $40 trillion. These figures are so immense that they are very difficult to imagine in a concrete manner; even though the amount of debt is so large that the numbers seem abstract, they are real and are the sign of a country in bad financial shape. All of these numbers for these three categories—the economy, unemployment, and debt—show that the United States of America really is in a state of emergency. With these tremendous problems going on, the solution for many people, especially those with the determination, perseverance, and talent or skill to do it, is to become entrepreneurs and start their own businesses, which we will explore further. (The good news is that you can learn many of the skills to become an entrepreneur on your own, even if they were not part of your education.)

3

ENTREPRENEURSHIP

What Is Entrepreneurship?

Entrepreneurship is the process of beginning a business and, through that business, offering a product or service that consumers can choose to purchase. Instead of working for another company, for example, entrepreneurs can work for themselves. Depending on the type of businesses that they start or join, people can work totally by themselves or can work collaboratively with business partners. There are almost an infinite number of businesses that entrepreneurs can become involved in.

Benefits of Entrepreneurship

While it may seem scary and like a huge risk, which it can be, entrepreneurship has many benefits. Think about this:

According to medical statistics, the percentage of people who have heart attacks increases by around 35 percent on Mondays. While it is impossible to say with certainty, what might be inferred from this is that more people have heart attacks on Mondays because they are dreading going to their jobs. If you have been in the work force long enough, you can relate to the feeling of dreading waking up on Monday mornings and having to go to a job that you dislike. Unfortunately, many people feel stuck in jobs that they do not enjoy. (Of course, many people who work for other companies enjoy their careers as well.) As an entrepreneur, however, you can be your own boss. Imagine having that freedom!

MAKE MONEY THE NEW FASHION WAY

Being in business for yourself means that you can be creative and can decide in which directions you want your business to go. You can focus on earning money by utilizing skills and talents or by selling products about which you are truly passionate. While there is risk involved in starting your own business or working as an independent contractor, there are also many potential rewards, such as the chance to earn more money than you ever dreamed possible while working when you want. I will not pretend that being in business for yourself is easy, because it is not, but the freedom that you have working for yourself is difficult to imagine if you've never been in the situation. As an entrepreneur, you make the decisions about the work you do and about your business; you do not have to ask permission from your boss because you are your own boss.

Moving Forward

Being in business for yourself is hard work, but, as discussed earlier, it has many benefits. At this point, assess yourself to see if being an entrepreneur is right for you.

Ask yourself these questions:

- Would you like not having a boss?
- Would you like to be your own boss?
- Would you enjoy setting your own work hours?
- Would you like not having an income limit?

- Would you be excited about taking vacations when you wanted?
- Do you want to "recession proof" your own life?
- Do you want to have more spare time?
- Would you like to retire your parents from work?
- If you decided to, would you like to be able to retire early?
- When you retire, would you like to be able to maintain a high standard of living?
- Do you want the tax incentives that come with owning your own business?
- Do you want financial freedom?
- Do you want to earn extra income?

If you said yes to the majority of these questions, then maybe being an entrepreneur is the right path for you. If you decide to become an entrepreneur, the next decision you will have to make is what kind of business you want to go into. To decide what type of business to pursue, you will want to look at several different factors, such as what your skills and abilities are, what kind of services or products you are interested in offering, and what your passions are. Entrepreneurs need to be visionaries who can see potential and tap into it. Let's look next at one particular type of business, network marketing, which has all of the above benefits and more!

4

Network Marketing

What Is Network Marketing?

Network marketing is a successful business model that allows companies to sell their products or services directly to consumers and helps them become distributors. It is called "network marketing" because the distributors form the network through which the company's products or services are sold. Another name for this highly successful business model is multilevel marketing. Through network marketing, the company provides its distributors with training, professional development, and support. What makes network marketing unique is that not only are network marketers able to make money selling the products or services themselves, but they also make money through the sales of the people who sell the product or service under them—those whom the network marketers sponsor and to whom they act as uplines. The fact that you can earn exponential profits is just one of the benefits of network marketing, which has some benefits that traditional businesses do not have.

Benefits of Network Marketing

There is some overlap in the benefits of being an entrepreneur and being a network marketer; however, network marketing has its own unique and compelling set of benefits. First, with network marketing, there is the potential to earn exponential profit. You can earn money from the sales you make as well as from the distributors who are signed up under you and the distributors who are signed up under them. Second, there are not the same risks of liability as there are with traditional businesses. Third, network marketing does not require as much capital as do traditional businesses. To open a brick-and-mortar restaurant, for example, your costs could easily be $200,000 or more. With network marketing, you can avoid the cost of a building and many of the other costs that people often incur when they start a traditional business. Fourth, it is much quicker and easier to get into a network-marketing business than it is to start a traditional business. If you were to start a traditional business, you would have to worry about obtaining an LLC, a trademark, and permits; having a building constructed or buying or renting office space; choosing a reputable lawyer; hiring an accountant and employees; and complying with local, state, and federal laws and regulations about businesses. When you become a network marketer, the company for whom you are distributing will worry about all of these things so that you don't have to. Fifth, through network marketing, you can acquire extra capital to pursue other interests or to support careers in which you may find it challenging to earn the money you need, such as music, acting, or art. (More than 80 percent of women in the United States who earn salaries of six figures or more a year achieve this through network marketing.) Sixth, through network marketing, you get many personal benefits, such as gaining or improving leadership skills, self-development, and personal growth; building skills in sales; increasing your emotional intelligence; and having the chance to help other people. For me, going into network marketing made sense because I wanted to earn more money and gain control of my time and life, and I wanted to be able to spend more time with family. In addition, I gained multiple personal benefits because of the excellent personal development offered through the network-marketing company with which I am involved. While it took some time to research and to consider all the pros and cons, I can say that network marketing was definitely the right choice for me; it might be for you as well!

Choosing the Right Network-Marketing Company

There are many network-marketing companies. As with most other things, not all of them are reputable or effective. And not all of them will be of interest to you. You have to make sure that you choose the right one for you—one that feels right and that lines up with products or services about which you feel passionate. Here are some factors to consider when choosing a network-marketing company to join. Do intensive online searches to find out information about the company, not only on the company website but also on other websites. See what kinds of comments people are making about the company. Talk to people who are involved with the company, whether you see them in person, e-mail them, call them, or communicate with them on social media; see what actual network marketers for the company have to say about it. What kind of reputation does the company have? How long has it been in business? What kind of investment is required up front or as you go along? Does the company have a rewarding compensation plan? Does it have team bonuses? Is it distributor driven? As noted earlier, one major difference between a traditional business and network marketing is the small amount of capital needed to get into network marketing.

Also, what kinds of development and training are available for distributors? High-quality network-marketing companies offer their network marketers extensive training. If you have little or no experience in sales, that is not a problem. The network-marketing company that you choose, if it is a worthwhile one, will provide you with training on how to market its products and services. Once you have chosen your network-marketing company, then it will be time to get to work learning all you can about the company, selling the company's products or services, and developing your list of prospects.

5

Prospecting

Create Your List

As you work to create your list of prospects to whom you are going to present your business opportunity, whether you have them in mind as clients who will buy from you, as potential distributors, or both, remember that the point is to find contacts who are appropriate and would likely be beneficial to your business. Your cell phone's list of contacts is one important source. Your social media accounts are also places to find contacts. E-mail lists and contact lists within e-mail accounts are additional sources of potential prospects. Also, the people around you—those with whom you work, as well as friends and family—are other possible contacts.

Keep in mind that you should narrow down your list of contacts instead of just blindly contacting everyone possible.

Also, make sure that you do not contact the same people through different methods with the same pitch; for example, some of your contacts on social media may also be listed in your e-mail or phone contacts. Also, consider what types of people you want to contact as potential prospects. What qualities are important to you for prospects? You may want people who have strong personalities, who get along well with others, who are smart, and who could help form the foundation of an effective team, for example. People who are go-getters should be at the very top of your list; you will probably want to contact people like this first. That's what I did, and it definitely helped me to form a strong and successful team. You may also want to ask other distributors within the network-marketing company, including your upline, about the types of people they contacted and what characteristics are desirable for potential distributors.

Network and Connect

Some people have three to four hundred people to sort through as they choose whom to contact as potential prospects. Other people may only have fifteen, twenty, or thirty people. Start with the people you know. As your business and network expands, so will the list of people you can approach. Also, as your business grows and as you get increasing numbers of distributors under you, your network will grow even more. Remember that every new prospect that one of the network marketers under you signs up will be added to your network. This means that your network can increase exponentially! The more people signed up under you, the faster and wider your own network will grow. If you are looking for good ways to find more people to connect with, consider attending events sponsored by organizations like your local chamber of commerce. There are also websites through which you can create meet-up groups and find other people with an interest in, or possible interest in, network marketing. You may also want to go to trade shows and other business-oriented events, especially in major cities if possible, to build more relationships with potential clients or distributors. These are all ways in which I have increased the size and scope of my network. You can do the same. The more that you interact with people about your business opportunity, the easier it gets.

INVITE

Soon you will have a working list of contacts. (Remember that even if people say no initially, it might be a good idea to follow up with them in a few months; you may even want to ask people who say they are not interested if you can contact them again several months down the road or ask for referrals.) Once you know whom you want to approach as potential prospects, figure out what you need to do next. The company for whom you are working as a network marketer, including your upline, should be able to give you guidance as you go through every step of the process. You may decide to set up a conference call with an upline at a certain time with each prospect. Depending on the company, you may be able to e-mail the prospects a video about the company once you have established their interest. You can set up a call, a video meeting, an online meeting, or a face-to-face meeting to help facilitate your prospects' decisions, which we will discuss further. Multiple exposures are more effective than just a single exposure in helping prospects decide to become a client (which means they will purchase the company's product directly from you) or a distributor (which means they will join your team, under you, as a network marketer). You want to build and increase the prospects' interest level in joining you. Utilize good timing. Keep the company and the prospective sales and profit opportunity somewhat of a mystery before you present the prospect with detailed information in order to increase anticipation with interest.

Here is an example of gradually working to increase a prospect's interest: First, call the prospect and introduce the business idea in general terms. Then, if the prospect seems interested, invite the person to an event or send the prospect information through e-mail about the company and its opportunities. (Consider asking the prospect what he or she likes best about the company's opportunity.) Then you should follow up with a three-way call including you, your prospect, and someone from your upline.

6

Present the Opportunity

Your Thirty-Second Story

Now that you have contacted people who may be interested in your product, service, or business opportunity and presented prospects with more information, it is time to give them your thirty-second story. This is your personal story that summarizes you and your situation. Your thirty-second story conveys to your listeners how you became involved in the product, service, or business opportunity and how it has changed your life for the better. Your story should have an emotional element to it that will cause listeners to be attentive and engaged; your story will help them relate their own experiences and needs to their interest in your product, service, or business opportunity.

Every person's thirty-second story is different. Your story will be exactly the same each time you tell it (you may have a version for the business opportunity and one for the product or service), and it should become second nature to you before long. In sales one thing to remember is that the first thirty seconds are the most important to sealing (or not sealing) a deal. Therefore, your personal story should be believable and interesting, and you should tell it with high energy, conviction, and enthusiasm in a way that is natural. Make sure your thirty-second story does not seem scripted. Your thirty-second story should be of interest to prospects who may become distributors and to those who may just buy the product or service your network-marketing company sells. It is important that before you begin telling your thirty-second story, you practice it with a few people, such as friends and family who are not prospects or with a business associate, such as an upline, just to make sure that it sounds believable—which it should be, because your story should be true and authentic. The more you practice, the better you will get, as with other aspects of network marketing.

Use a Tool

When you find people who are interested, you will need to be able to give them accurate and specific information about the network-marketing company. One way to do this is through the use of tools. Reputable network-marketing companies have tools that network marketers can use to explain their business and products or services clearly to interested prospects. The tools can be in a wide variety of formats, such as DVDs,

CDs, online videos, e-mails, magazines, and even 1-800 telephone numbers with prerecorded material. Another possible tool to use is the three-way call with you, your upline, and a prospect; we will discuss this more in detail in Chapter 7. Whatever tool or tools you choose, make sure to match the tool with the prospect and his or her individual preferences or learning styles.

Know Your Presentation

After your prospects have heard your thirty-second story and have been provided with tools to give them further information about the network-marketing company, you will be in the position to give your own presentation, including answering questions from prospects. There may be a home presentation (either in your home, a business associate's home, or a prospect's home), a one-on-one meeting in a public location (such as a coffee shop), or a phone or online meeting. You may want to bring in your upline, through Skype or other means, at some point during the presentation. Make sure that your presentation is organized and that you have tried it out on other nonprospects, such as associates or friends and family; it is always best to practice and polish presentations and improve them if needed before you present to prospects. When you do give your presentations, make sure that your thoughts are in order. Also, exude excitement and positive energy, as your prospects will sense and react to your energy. A presentation might consist, for example, of showing a short video and explaining further about the company and how you became involved in it. Then, you should ask the prospects what their personal and professional goals are. You should explain further about the benefits of the product, service, or business opportunity offered by the company and then ask the prospects what they like best about the company so far (to elicit positive thoughts and responses). Another idea is to present prospects, especially those only interested in purchasing the product or service, with the idea of how to get their products or services paid for by becoming a distributor. The goal of the presentation is to create excitement among prospects. Do make sure to share your personal story, tell the truth, and be compliant with the company's standards, vision, and expectations.

7

Fortune Is in the Follow-Up

Follow Up

Once you have given your prospects your thirty-second story, provided them with one or more tools, and presented to them, it will be time to follow up. Keep in mind that following up with a prospect is extremely important for several reasons. Following up shows that you are trustworthy, because you do what you say you are going to do, and it gives prospects the chance to consider how your product, service, or business opportunity could improve their lives. Also, it may take several exposures and tries before a prospect decides to sign up. Depending on your prospects and their level of interest, you may have to follow up multiple times, anywhere from two to ten. Patience and understanding that it may take several attempts to get someone on board are, therefore, essential. You want to follow up with the prospects as soon as possible after the initial meeting. Plant seeds to encourage their interest by asking positively slanted questions, such as, "What did you like best about the information I gave you?" or "Are you interested in learning more about how to recession proof your lifestyle?" Instead of talking too much, make sure that you actually listen to your prospect. If you are on a telephone call with your prospect and he or she sounds negative and not interested, you can end the call and schedule a follow-up for some time in the near future (if you think the prospect might change his or her mind). If people are interested in the business and in becoming distributors, send them more information, such as videos on the compensation plan. If they are more interested in the product or service, send them more videos and information on the product or service. If they want to sign up right away, help them to do so, and show them the back office (or the website) from the user's perspective. The bottom line for following up is that if you say you are going to meet them at a coffee shop or online at a certain time, do so. The most important part of the process is not pressuring a prospect to sign up as a customer or distributor but instead to build a relationship with him or her that will, hopefully, turn into a long-term one.

Three-Way Call

When you have interested prospects, one method you can use that often helps increase their interest is the three-way call. The purpose of a three-way call is, like other methods, to give prospects more information about the company, so they can make informed decisions about whether network marketing is right for them. A three-way call is between you, your upline, and the prospect. Before you begin the substantive portion of the conversation, you will want to go through a process called edification. You will edify (in other words, praise and uplift) your upline, whom you may want to refer to as your business partner. For example, you might say something like, "Shirley is one of my business partners who has helped mentor me and many others on our team. Shirley is a great leader and always leads by example. She has been in this business for more than fifteen years, has thousands of distributors in her organization, and has earned several million dollars because of her skill, dedication, and consistency and her ability to teach the process of duplication." Speaking highly of your upline is a reliable way of increasing the upline's credibility to your prospect. After you do this, your upline should, in turn, edify you. The reason for edification is to show the prospect that both you and your upline are credible and trustworthy by building each other up. Once that has occurred—and it must, since it is an integral part of a three-way call—let your upline present the prospect with more information about the company, and let the prospect ask questions. You will also want to ask the prospect questions; again, asking questions that are framed in a positive manner will help to elicit more positive responses. Note that you should make sure that your upline knows you will be calling and is in place before you begin the three-way call with your prospect.

Neutralize Objections

As you work through the process of trying to educate a prospective network marketer (or customer) to become involved with your company, you will invariably run into objections. Prospects who are somewhat interested in your product, service, or business opportunity can come up with all sorts of reasons why they can't or shouldn't or won't get involved. While some of these reasons may well be valid, as a network marketer trying to expand your number of downlines who are distributing, you will want to neutralize these objections when possible. Note that your responses to these concerns should not be condescending or dismissive. Instead of trying to prove that the prospects' concerns are invalid and ridiculous, which will not help to get them on board, you should instead respectfully and unemotionally provide logical responses for them that will help convince them that their objections are groundless.

Here are some potential responses to prospects' objections, questions, or concerns:

1. Prospect's concern: "This costs too much."

    Your response: This may be a particular concern for customers who want to buy the product (who may later turn into network marketers themselves), but it can certainly be a concern for potential network marketers or distributors as well. If the product is a cleanse and meal-replacement system, for example, help prospects look at the situation rationally. If they don't think they can afford $300 per month for a meal replacement system, help them calculate the amount of money they currently spend on food and then compare that to the monthly cost of the product. Show them that they are simply going to be reallocating the money they would normally spend on groceries and eating meals out to the meal replacement system. Prospects may not have thought of it in this way. If the amount still strikes them as too high, consider suggesting a cheaper monthly alternative if there is one, such as buying a different system.

2. Prospect's concern: "I don't have time to do this."

    Your response: Tell the prospects that while you completely understand their concern, you have found that distributors can work on the business part time, devoting small increments of time here and there, and still make progress.

3. Prospect's concern: "How much money have you made?"

    Your response: If you have made a great deal of money with network marketing, you can tell them so. If not, you can explain that you are still building up your business and that, if they would like, you can set up a three-way call with a business partner who has made a lot of money with network marketing.

4. Prospect's concern: "I am just not good at sales."

    Your response: Explain that you really do not know many people who are natural salespeople and that network marketing is more about attracting people to positive business situations, providing leadership, and helping people meet their goals. It is more about relationship building with people they know and meet than selling products or services.

5. Prospect's concern: "Is this a pyramid scheme?"

    Your response: Ask them what their definition of a pyramid scheme is. Invariably, their definition will not coincide with what network marketing truly is. Explain that pyramid schemes are illegal and that they are not something you would be involved with.

8

THE DECISION

Emotionally Detach from the Outcome

It is essential that, as you work through the process of informing and eliciting interest and involvement from prospects, you not have an emotional attachment to their decisions if they decide they are not interested. If a person does not sign up, there are other leads you can follow; this is a process of sifting and sorting. You are, in a way, interviewing prospects to see if they are qualified and a good fit for your organization. If you are emotionally detached from the outcome, you will avoid wasting the time and energy you might spend worrying about why a prospect chose not to become involved.

Ask Questions

Gauge where prospects are at in terms of their interest. By this point in the process, you should have some idea of the level of interest of your prospects; however, it is useful to ask them specific questions to find this out. While you may be very accurate in your assessment of prospects' interest and plans, you may be surprised to find out that some of them are much more interested or much less interested than you thought. Ask them questions about their lives and about how network marketing would fit into their lives and their goals. These questions should be asked of all prospects, not just those who are definitely interested and have already signed up. Here are some possible questions to ask: What are your goals? How do you plan to reach these goals? What kind of retirement do you envision for yourself? If you could do anything now, what would you want to do? What do you want out of life? On a scale of one to ten, with ten being the most comfortable, how comfortable are you with making a decision about this opportunity? If a prospect gives an answer of seven or less, you may want to send him or her more information. Remember that it is often a good idea to ask positively framed questions, such as what excites the prospect about network marketing and the opportunities it provides. Make sure that you listen carefully to the answers; listening is just as important as talking, if not more so, in situations such as this. Your questions, if asked skillfully, will help the prospect to reflect on his or her interest and to make a decision of some type.

Close

Trying to close is often where people mess up. Some people will already know what they want and will have signed up by this point. Most people, however, will be somewhat undecided and will need some direction. If you don't know exactly how to close, you can always ask your upline for support. Make a suggestion if your prospects are open to it; what do you think would fit them? If your prospects are unsure, ask if you can give them a recommendation. If so, then assess their strengths and interests and make a suggestion. If they are very knowledgeable and interested, for example, you might recommend that they become distributors. Prospects who seem more interested in just the products or services, however, might be good candidates to sign up as customers (who might become network marketers later). As always, do not hesitate to ask your upline for assistance. If you are not experienced enough to close yet, you might even get your upline on a three-way call. Throughout the process, remain confident and maintain good energy. Close if the prospects are sure of what they want. If they aren't, you can always utilize another tool to give them more information.

9

Mentoring

Upline Support

At all levels of network marketing, mentorship is an important element. Mentoring is important and helps you become a leader. You will receive mentorship and support from your upline, and you will mentor your downlines, the distributors who signed up under you. As an upline to your distributors (and as a product/service expert for your customers), you are also acting as a mentor and, therefore, as a leader. Gaining confidence as a leader will also help improve your skills as a mentor. You will gain valuable leadership skills from your upline. One necessary aspect of providing upline support is to teach your distributors to duplicate the processes and systems for training and sales that the network-marketing company already has in place.

The ability to utilize these processes and systems is absolutely essential to success in network marketing. You must also be able to train your distributors to sign up other customers and distributors under them and to set and meet goals for rank advancements and lead generation. Train them to set goals such as contacting a certain number of prospects each month. Teach them to use tools such as three-way calls. Set them up for success. Your distributors should be able to rely on you as their upline, especially after you get the hang of things, just as you rely on your upline. You can learn from three-way calls and events how to mentor your downlines. Above all, you want to provide moral support and build a team culture of success.

Events

One way to build motivation and increase inspiration within your team is to bring them to events. Events give the team a chance to come together. They also provide camaraderie. Events build trust and belief in the network-marketing process and provide a mechanism for accountability and for the celebration of achievement.

There are two main types of events. One type of event presents the opportunity for network marketing with your company. At these events, it is useful to bring one or more potentially interested distributors so that you can help guide them toward signing up and joining your team. You want to be selective, of course, about whom you invite, making sure to bring prospects who are motivated and positive. At these events, network marketers who are successful will speak about their experiences; also, presentations about opportunities for network marketing (and making money) with the company are given.

Another type of event is a network-marketing company's conference or meeting, where the company provides training events and individual or team recognition. There may be a big meeting each year and several smaller ones throughout the year. Besides bringing members of your team to events such as this, you should also bring at least one prospect as your guest who you believe has the potential to be successful and who is highly motivated. In addition to training your team, these events help to build credibility and belief in the system.

Self-Development

Whether you are in network marketing or some other field, it is important and beneficial to work toward continually improving as a person and to learn new skills. There is always a reason to diversify your skills and experience and to focus on learning and on new ways of thinking about life. Below is a list of books that I would recommend that you read for your personal development, to help you become more well rounded in life and as a network marketer. I have read each one of these books and have found all of them to be useful in my journey toward increasing my development and, in turn, my personal growth; I learned something important from each one of these books.

1. *The Law of Success* (original 1925 edition), by Napoleon Hill

2. *The Science of Mind: The Complete Edition*, by Ernest Holmes

3. *The 7 Habits of Highly Effective People*, by Stephen R. Covey

4. *The 8th Habit: From Effectiveness to Greatness*, by Stephen R. Covey

5. *Think and Grow Rich*, by Napoleon Hill

6. *Rich Dad, Poor Dad*, by Robert T. Kiyosaki

7. *Becoming a Person of Influence: How to Positively Impact the Lives of Others*, by John C. Maxwell and Jim Dornan

8. *How to Win Friends and Influence People*, by Dale Carnegie

9. *Ice Breakers! How to Get Any Prospect to Beg You for a Presentation*, by Tom "Big Al" Schreiter

10. *How to Get Instant Trust, Belief, Influence, and Rapport!* by Tom "Big Al" Schreiter

I would suggest that you read all of the books listed above. (I have read some of them multiple times and found that I get something new out of them each time I read them.) Also, think of other books you've read that you would add to a list like this. You may find yourself recommending some of these or other books to your downlines. You might even want to consider developing your own list of books, which could include any of these, to give the network marketers who are signed up under you.

10

The Journey

Enjoy the Journey

It is very important that you enjoy the journey and are grateful for it. Enjoy your training, your work, and your life. If you don't enjoy the journey, you are really missing out. The entire journey should be an adventure. By the way, you may discover after being in network marketing for a while that you are enjoying your personal journey even more than you were before. If, before network marketing, you felt stuck in a career that you did not like, and after starting network marketing, you get much more satisfaction out of your journey, this is probably an indication that you have made the right decision. Change can be scary, but it is often worth it.

Enjoying your challenges as well as your successes will help you to grow as a businessperson and as an individual. If you enjoy what you are doing, you will more than likely be able to improve as a person, an entrepreneur, a leader, a salesperson, and a mentor. You can become a more positive person. It is a good feeling when you can help someone with a high-quality product or service. It is also a good feeling when you help one of your distributors to achieve success on the business side, which means that he or she has earned more money and more freedom. Embrace the now, both in the present and in the future. You never know where you'll go or whom you will meet in the exciting world of network marketing.

Help Others

In business, you need to be of the mind-set to help others. If you have this mind-set, then you have almost no choice but to succeed. If your only focus is on making money, you will miss important aspects of network marketing, such as the joy that comes from helping people and the importance of providing the best customer service and mentorship possible. The whole process of network marketing is rewarding. People signed under you start making money, so you are helping them financially. People buying from you and your distributors are helped by a quality product or service that improves their lives. You can be proud of changing someone's life for the better. Appreciate the opportunity to give back to society. To achieve success in any business, you must be willing to help others and have a mind-set of gratitude for the opportunity to help. If you are only in it for the money, you are likely not helping yourself or anyone else. There is almost always a benefit that comes from striving to help other people; the money will naturally flow from the work that you do to help others in network marketing.

Personal Growth

Self-development involves reading books and doing things that will help you grow and learn. Personal growth, on the other hand, is the result of self-development. Reflect on how you've grown through the whole process in terms of relationships and the benefits to your personal life and professional life. Growth happens organically and is due to learning and allowing yourself to expand your knowledge and skills and improve as a person. Growth is a lifelong process. You should always keep growing and blossoming. It is likely that you will gain skills and derive benefits from your journey as a network marketer that you did not imagine in the beginning. While the process is different for each person, depending on his or her needs and experiences, here are some possible benefits that indicate personal growth and that you could gain from network marketing: increased self-esteem, improved motivation, self-actualization (in other words, becoming the best person that you can and meeting your goals, resulting in fulfillment), increased happiness, a better outlook on life, more satisfaction with your work and life, and new (and improved) interpersonal relationships.

Your Destiny

Your destiny begins now! This is where you explore your options according to your wants, needs, and comfort zone to create the world of your dreams. This is the time for change to develop the entrepreneur in you. Map out a new, successful *now*, and remember to be positive and persistent. The time is now!

Affirmation Bonus Chapter

I Am the Force

IN THIS CHAPTER we will discuss the power of affirmations for success and overall well-being. The power of "I am" is truly amazing. By claiming "I am" in your affirmations, you are declaring desires as already true. Affirmations are a form of self-hypnosis. The more the affirmations are repeated on a daily basis, the more the subconscious mind believes they are actually true.

It is important to say affirmations at least twice a day—when you first wake up and right before you go to sleep—and to take a few minutes to visualize them as well. Affirmations should be spoken both aloud and silently in your mind for best results. When you are by yourself, you can say the affirmations out loud; if you want to continue to reinforce the affirmations throughout the day, you can say them silently in your mind.

MAKE MONEY THE NEW FASHION WAY

The subconscious mind has many filters that need to be penetrated in order to plant the seeds of the results you desire. The mind cannot tell the difference between imagination and reality, which is why imagination and visualization are so important in this process. See yourself in your visualizations, almost as if you are watching a movie in which you are the star.

It is essential that you have a positive attitude during this process. Your actions should be aligned with your recurring thoughts. Both of these steps will speed up the process. Once both of these steps occur, the mind starts to emit those thoughts as frequencies out to the universe. The universe then conspires to make those thoughts manifest. So behind the scenes, while you are living your life and applying these steps, the universe is coordinating to manifest your desires.

Pay attention to what happens around you, because everything is a sign and is attracted into your life from your thoughts. Your present reality is your past thoughts manifested. This has been known for many centuries, and numerous world leaders, including successful business leaders, have tapped into affirmations to achieve greatness.

Here we will break up these affirmations into a few sections. We will cover health, happiness, relationships, mental well-being, spiritual well-being, wealth creation, and success in network marketing. By working on improving all these areas of your life, you are planting the seeds of your future! Having all these areas work in harmony will bring great abundance in all aspects of your life.

You can choose to start in the area where you need help the most. I would recommend saying your chosen affirmations first thing in the morning and right before you go to bed. Repeat daily for the best results possible. Let's get started!

Affirmations for Health

- I am healthy.
- I am energetic.
- My whole body is perfect.
- Every cell in my body is perfect.
- My DNA is perfect.
- My cardiovascular system is 100 percent healthy.

- My digestive and excretory systems are 100 percent healthy.

- My endocrine and exocrine systems are 100 percent healthy.

- My skin is 100 percent healthy.

- My lymphatic and immune systems are 100 percent healthy.

- My musculoskeletal system is 100 percent healthy.

- My nervous system is 100 percent healthy.

- My urinary system is 100 percent healthy.

- My reproductive system is 100 percent healthy.

- My respiratory system is 100 percent healthy.

- All systems in my body are 100 percent healthy and working in harmony with each other.

MAKE MONEY THE NEW FASHION WAY

- I am youthful.
- With every step and breath I take, I get better and better in every possible way.
- I am one with the universe; therefore, my body is 100 percent healthy.
- I am in the best physical shape of my life.
- I feel amazing every single day.
- I am flexible.
- I am the perfect weight.
- I am ageless.
- I have perfect vision.
- I have perfect hearing.
- All of my organs work together in perfect harmony.
- My coordination is excellent.

- I am attractive to others.
- I am photogenic.
- I am playful.
- I have great balance.
- My skin and hair are youthful.
- I eat healthy foods.
- My actions are in line with my thoughts.

Affirmations for Happiness

- I am the creator of my dreams.
- I say what I mean, and I receive it.
- I am always happy.
- I always smile.

- I always laugh.
- I make people laugh.
- I am funny.
- I enjoy life.
- I wake up happy every morning.
- I am happy to help others.
- My journey through life is amazing.
- I am happy to be alive and well.
- I am happy that I have kind and generous people in my life.
- I am happy that I have an amazing family.
- I am happy that I love what I do for a living.
- I am happy to donate to my favorite charities.
- I am happy that I am successful.

- I am happy that I am financially free.
- My actions are in line with my thoughts.

Affirmations for Relationships

- All of my relationships—personal and business—are fulfilling.
- I am grateful for all the amazing relationships in my life.
- I am grateful for my significant other.
- I am grateful for my family.
- I am grateful for all the amazing business relationships I have.

- I always have great relationships with everyone who crosses my path.
- I possess amazing emotional intelligence.
- I am amazing at managing my emotions.
- Everyone I speak to appreciates me.
- I am always greeted with love, happiness, assistance, and cooperation.
- Everyone loves me.
- I am a people person.
- I always attract the right relationships into my life.
- All of my personal and business relationships benefit me.
- My actions are in line with my thoughts.

Affirmations for Mental Well-Being

- I have strength and willpower in all that I do.
- I am self-confident and have high self-esteem.
- I have a healthy balance between work, play, and rest.
- I have the flexibility to learn new things in life and adapt to change with ease.
- I am wise.
- I am calm.
- I have mental clarity.
- I am at ease.
- I am one with the universe.

MAKE MONEY THE NEW FASHION WAY

- I am witty.
- I am sharp.
- I am mentally strong.
- I am intelligent.
- I am great at troubleshooting.
- I am relaxed.
- I am patient.
- I have a great memory.
- I am focused.
- I have the answers.
- I always win.
- I am free.
- I am mentally fit.

- I have great intuition.
- I have perfect balance in all aspects of my life.
- My actions are in line with my thoughts.

Affirmations for Spiritual Well-Being

- I am eternal.
- My spirit and body are flawless.
- I am one with my god.
- I am one with the universe.
- I am at peace with who I am.
- I am in tune with my inner self.
- I always find the answers within myself.

- I love to meditate.
- My manifestations come true with ease.
- I surround myself with pure, clean energy.
- My energy is as pure as white light.
- I am spiritually inclined.
- I am the force.
- My actions are in line with my thoughts.

Affirmations for Wealth Creation

- I do what I love, and the money follows.
- I am successful in life.
- I am excellence personified.
- I am abundant in all aspects of my life.

- I am a money magnet daily.

- I attract money to myself every day.

- People love to give me money.

- People love to write me checks.

- I receive checks in the mail for very large amounts.

- Every day my bank account balance keeps growing.

- I make money while I sleep.

- I make money 24-7, 365 days a year.

- I love what I can do with all my money.

- I love that I can help people with my money.

- Money comes to me easily every day.

- I am one with this money.

- I am in perfect harmony with all this money.

- I make amazing investments with all my money.

- I am recession proof.

- I attract more and more money every day.

- I love to make large donations to charity to help others.

- My investments always have high returns.

- I am a multimillionaire, and I love it.

- My actions are in line with my thoughts.

Affirmations for Success in Network Marketing

- I love myself.

- I have great posture.

- I am confident and intelligent.

- I invite my prospects with ease.

- I have an amazing thirty-second story.
- I always use tools to best match my prospects.
- I am great at giving presentations.
- I am an expert at following up.
- I am a natural at three-way calls.
- I neutralize objections effectively.
- I am emotionally detached from the outcome.
- I close the deal.
- I ask the right questions at the right time.
- I give great upline support to my team.
- I go to events with prospects and team members to build belief and accountability.
- I am always working on self-development.
- I am enjoying the journey.

- I love helping others succeed in network marketing.
- I work well with others.
- I lead with emotional intelligence.
- I ask great questions.
- I am a great leader.
- I develop great leaders.
- I have a large organization in my network-marketing business.
- I constantly sign up business builders.
- I build my residual income daily.
- I am worthy of the best life has to offer.
- I receive abundance of the universe in every area of my life.
- I am the number-one income earner every year.

- I always get my downline continually paid.
- I help my team members advance quickly in rank, and they duplicate the process effectively.
- I attract the right prospects.
- The right prospects attract me.
- I am always receiving the right leads.
- I complete my tasks with speed, ease, and perfection.
- I am highly organized.
- I am highly motivated.
- I am a master listener.
- I am inspired.
- I inspire others.
- I am living the life of my dreams.
- My residual income increases every day.

MAKE MONEY THE NEW FASHION WAY

- I am helping hundreds of thousands of lives globally.
- I attract business builders.
- My team members share my values.
- I love speaking with new people every day.
- My network is growing rapidly every day.
- People have a need, and I have the answer.
- I have many millionaires in my downline.
- I am a multimillionaire.
- I always execute my tasks at hand.
- I am very detailed in my work.
- I have a great work ethic.
- I am an entrepreneur.
- I am making money the new-fashion way.
- I love network marketing.

- My list of prospects is always growing with business builders.
- I am a master of networking and relationship building.
- I connect easily with others.
- My actions are in line with my thoughts.

These are just some of the affirmations I apply daily to my life. You can always add to these affirmations as needed. Just remember to start with "I am" and always speak in the present tense. It is very important to remember that your actions are aligned with your thoughts. Being thankful for what you already have is very important in getting to the next level. Gratitude, giving, and being helpful to others are must-haves in order to succeed.

MAKE MONEY THE NEW FASHION WAY

As the well-known saying goes, you have to give to receive, that actually results from a very interesting principle. When you give to or help someone, your subconscious actually views it as receiving something yourself, since we are all one and connected to the universe. So the mind starts thinking of more abundance, and more abundance arrives. To be abundant in all aspects of your life is to be truly successful.

In this section you will create your own affirmations, or you can simply choose from the previous affirmations and write down the ones you desire the most. Each affirmation starts with "I am," and you will fill in the blanks.

- I am _____.

- I am _____.

- I am _____.

- I am _____.

- I am _____.

- I am _____.

- I am _____.

- I am _____.

- I am _____.

- I am _____.

- I am _____.

- I am _____.

- I am _____.

- I am _____.

- I am _____.

- I am _____.

- I am _____.

- I am _____.

- I am _____.

Daily Mantra Template

Below you will fill in the blanks for your daily mantra. Your mantra needs to be very detailed so that you can receive the specific items you desire.

MAKE MONEY THE NEW FASHION WAY

- I have _____

  _____ dollars liquid in my bank account.

- I provide the business service of _____

  _____

  _____ to achieve my financial goals.

- I donate large sums of money to _____

  _____

  _____, which is my favorite charity.

- I give back to society by _____

  _____

  _____

  _____.

- I love what I do because _____

  _____

_____

_____.

- I am grateful that my life is _____

_____

_____

_____.

- I am so happy that _____

_____

_____

_____.

- Being an entrepreneur has provided me with _____

_____

_____

_____.

- I make money the new-fashion way, and it allows me

  to _____

  _____

  _____

  _____.

- My residual income increases every day and excites

  me because _____

  _____

  _____

  _____.

NOTES

MAKE MONEY THE NEW FASHION WAY

_____

_____

_____

_____

About the Author

Ruben Cobos is a visionary business leader and savvy investor who has successfully founded and built numerous businesses across multiple sectors over the last twenty years. He is a motivational speaker and business consultant to numerous celebrity entertainers and entrepreneurs.

With a proven track record for personally generating more than $10 million in corporate sales, Mr. Cobos is an inspired leader who thrives in a team environment. With his powerful combination of business strengths in strategic planning, marketing and branding, public relations, project management, event planning, multimedia, and social media coupled with his genuine love of people and adept emotional intelligence, Ruben is able to motivate teams to exceptional success, having led teams that have managed more than $25 million in sales and events that have serviced more than 450,000 people.

Ruben is a serial entrepreneur who is an expert in the areas of multimedia, social media, Alexa ranking, search engine optimization, website creation, and Google AdWords to leverage the power of the Internet for both his own internal projects and businesses and his various business partnerships.

Mr. Cobos simultaneously launched his first record label, production company/recording studio, and music publishing company in 2001. He later went on to launch a second record label in 2003. He has received multiple awards for his record label/movement with established award shows in NYC, including Indie Label of the Year (2005) and CEO of the Year (2008).

In 2002 Ruben was presented with the Millionaire Elite award for his expertise in building a lucrative real estate portfolio.

In addition to his many business pursuits, Ruben is a writer and musician who is passionate about health, nutrition, spirituality, and personal development and who has a deep love of animals. His vision is to ultimately open a no-kill shelter.

www.ingramcontent.com/pod-product-compliance
Lightning Source LLC
Chambersburg PA
CBHW060517030426
42337CB00015B/1927